MORE WATERCOLOR
WHIMSY FROM
LAUREL NELSON

FOR
ANDREW CUMMINS

THANK YOU

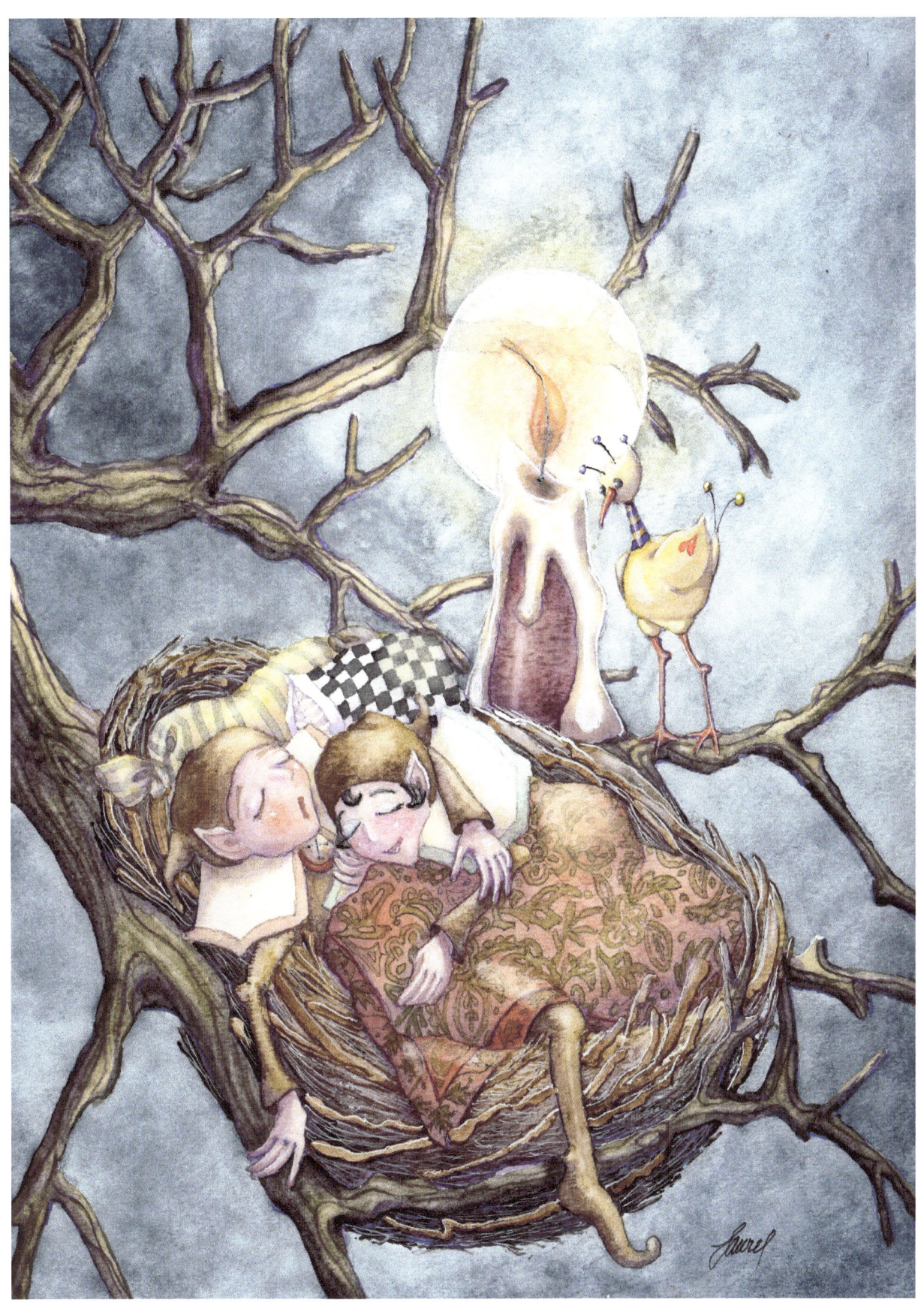

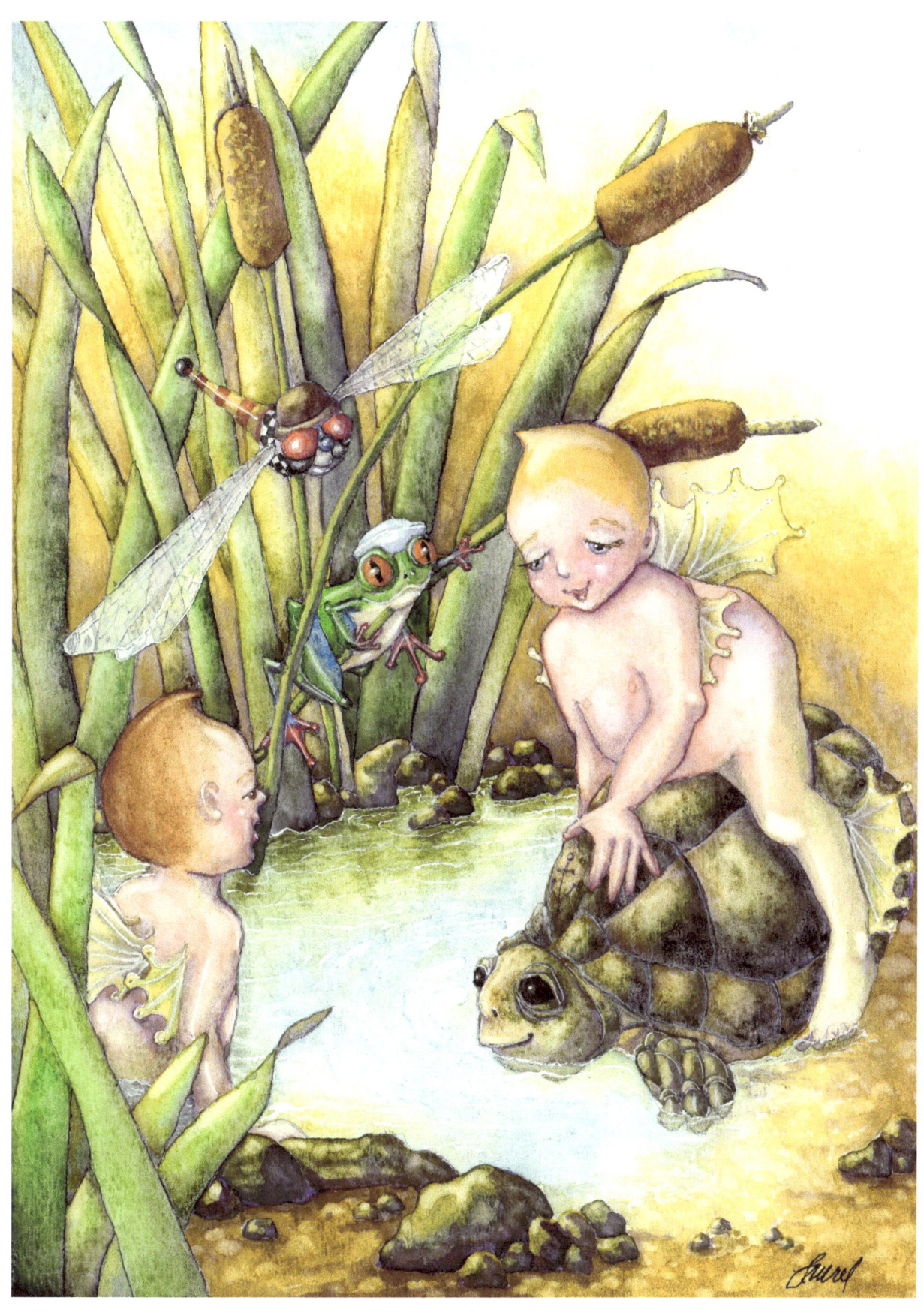

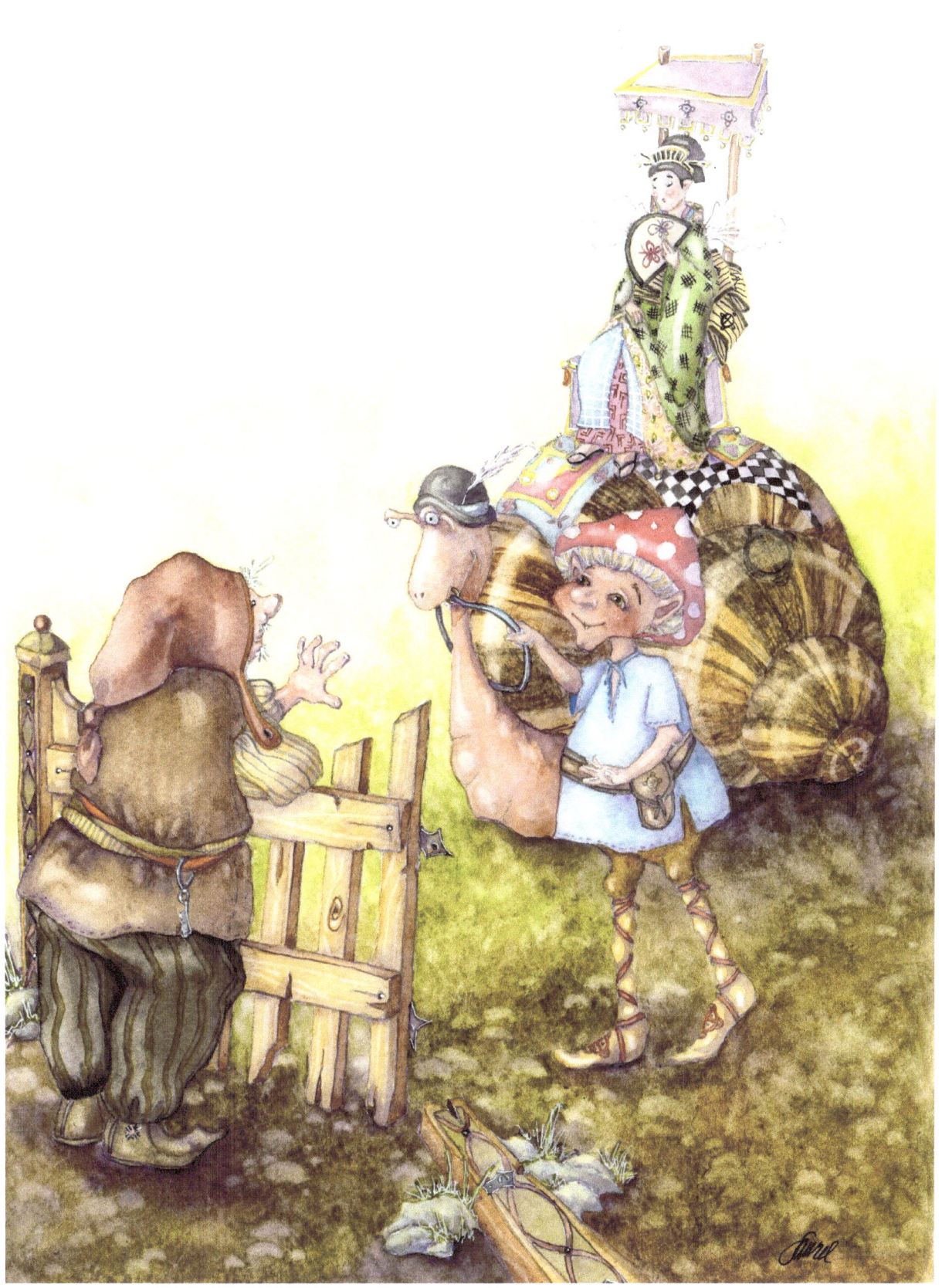

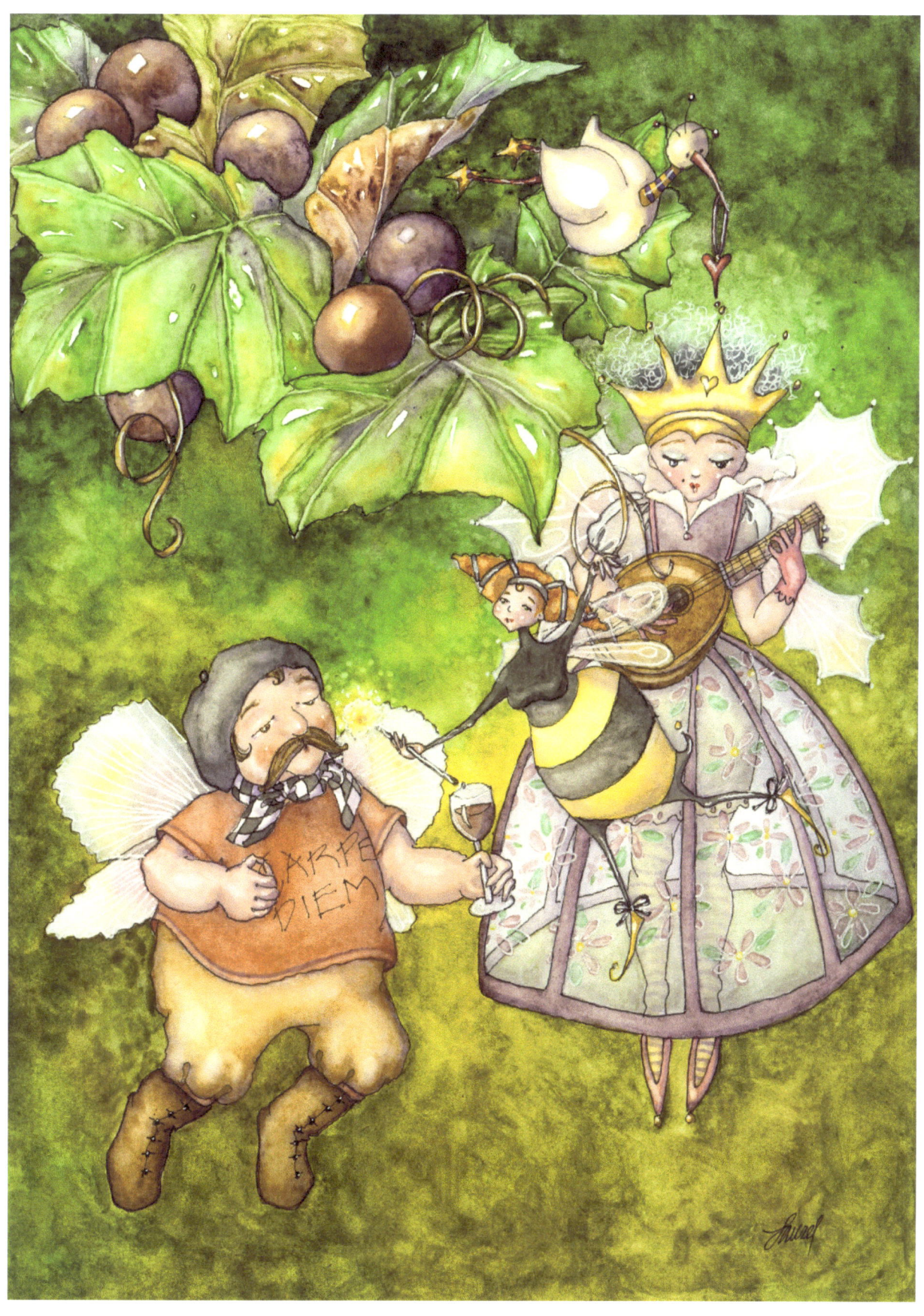

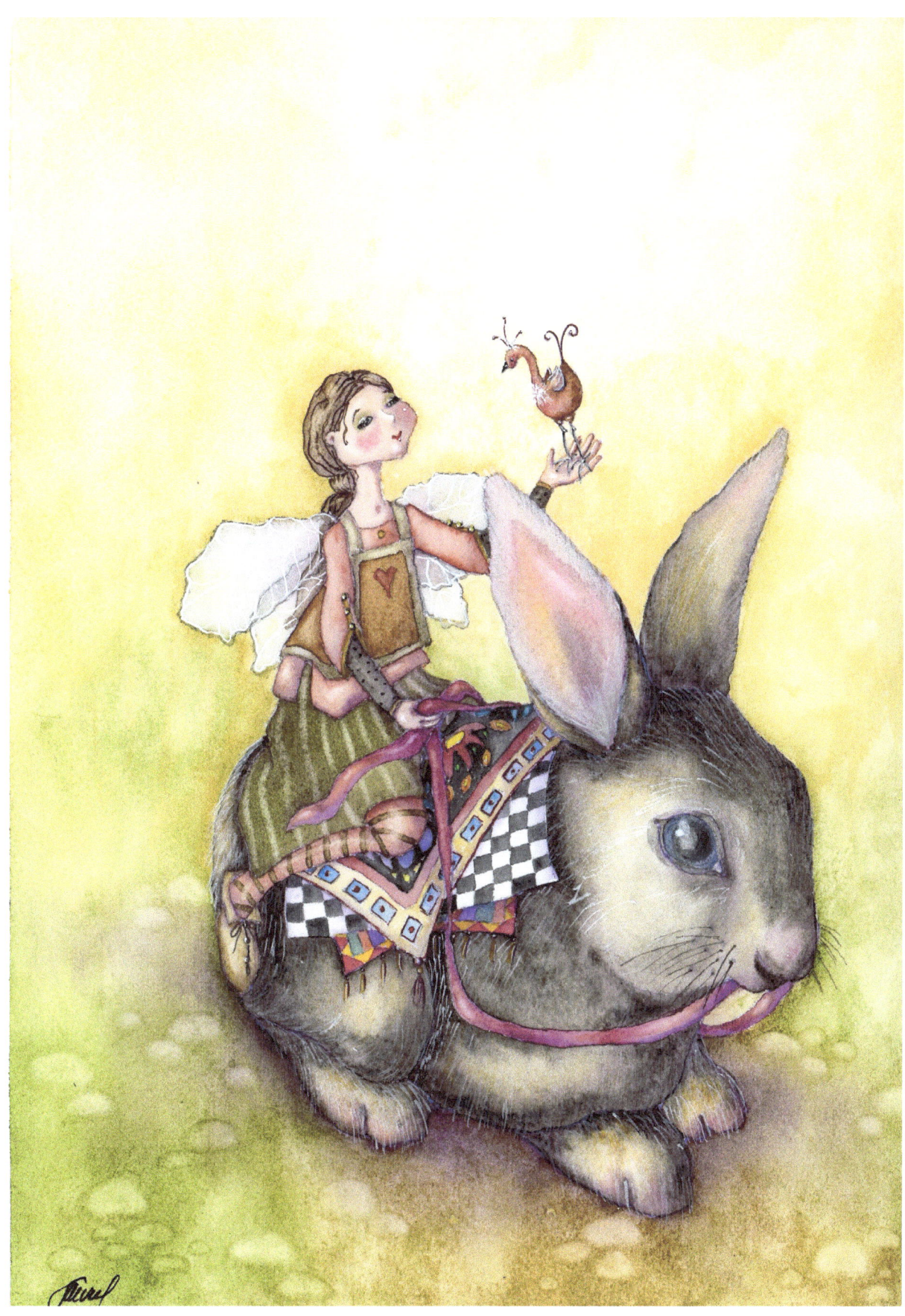

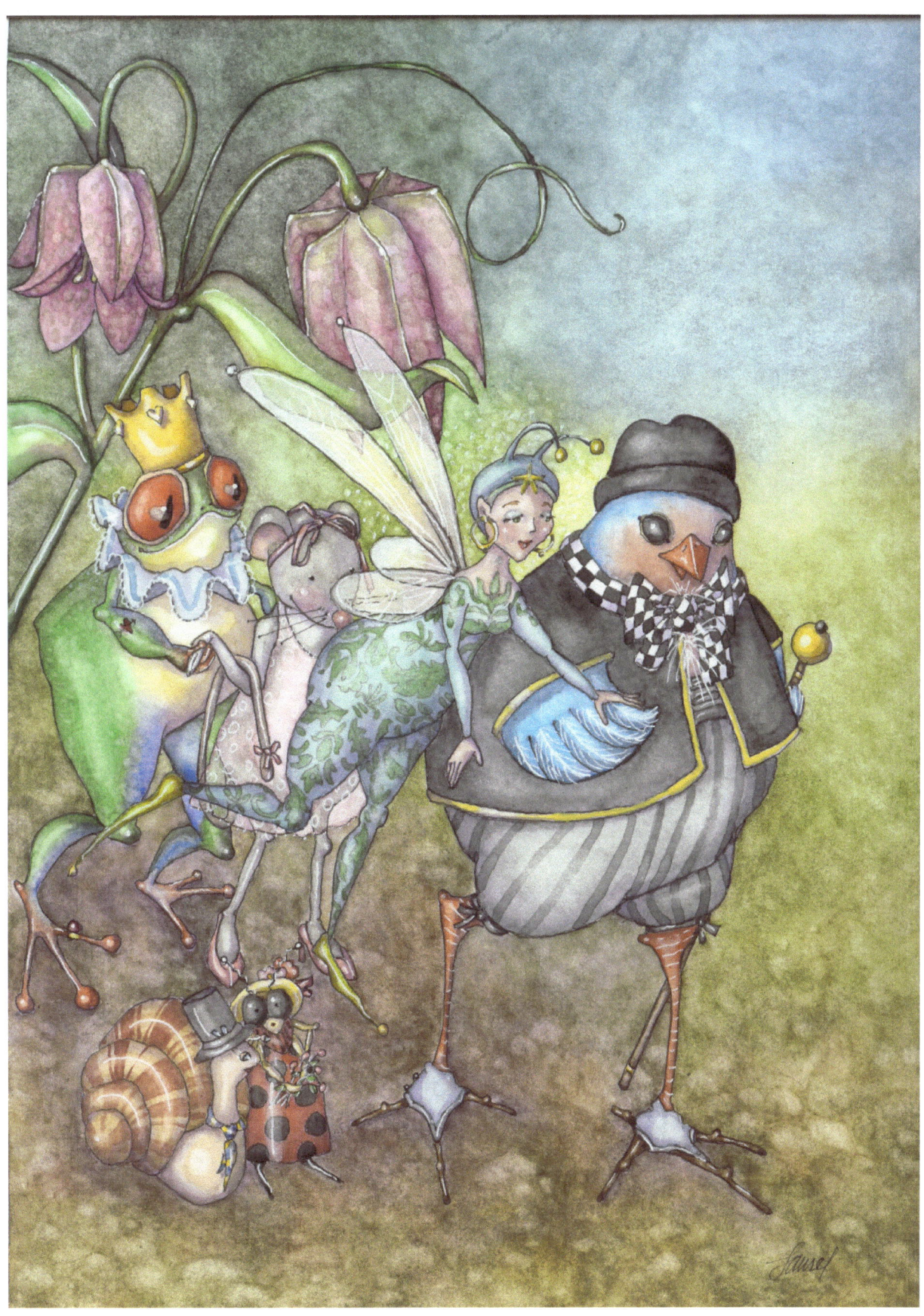

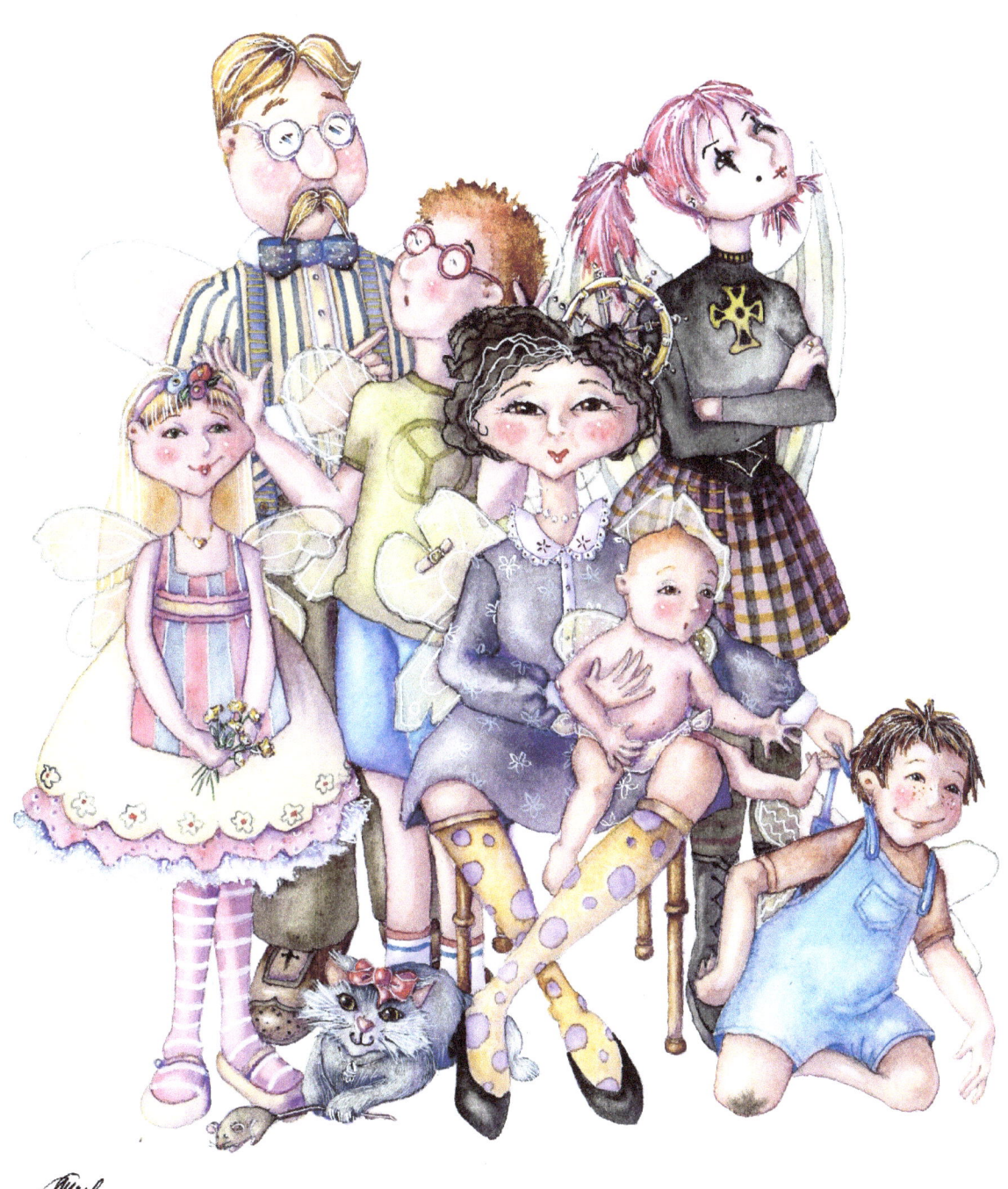

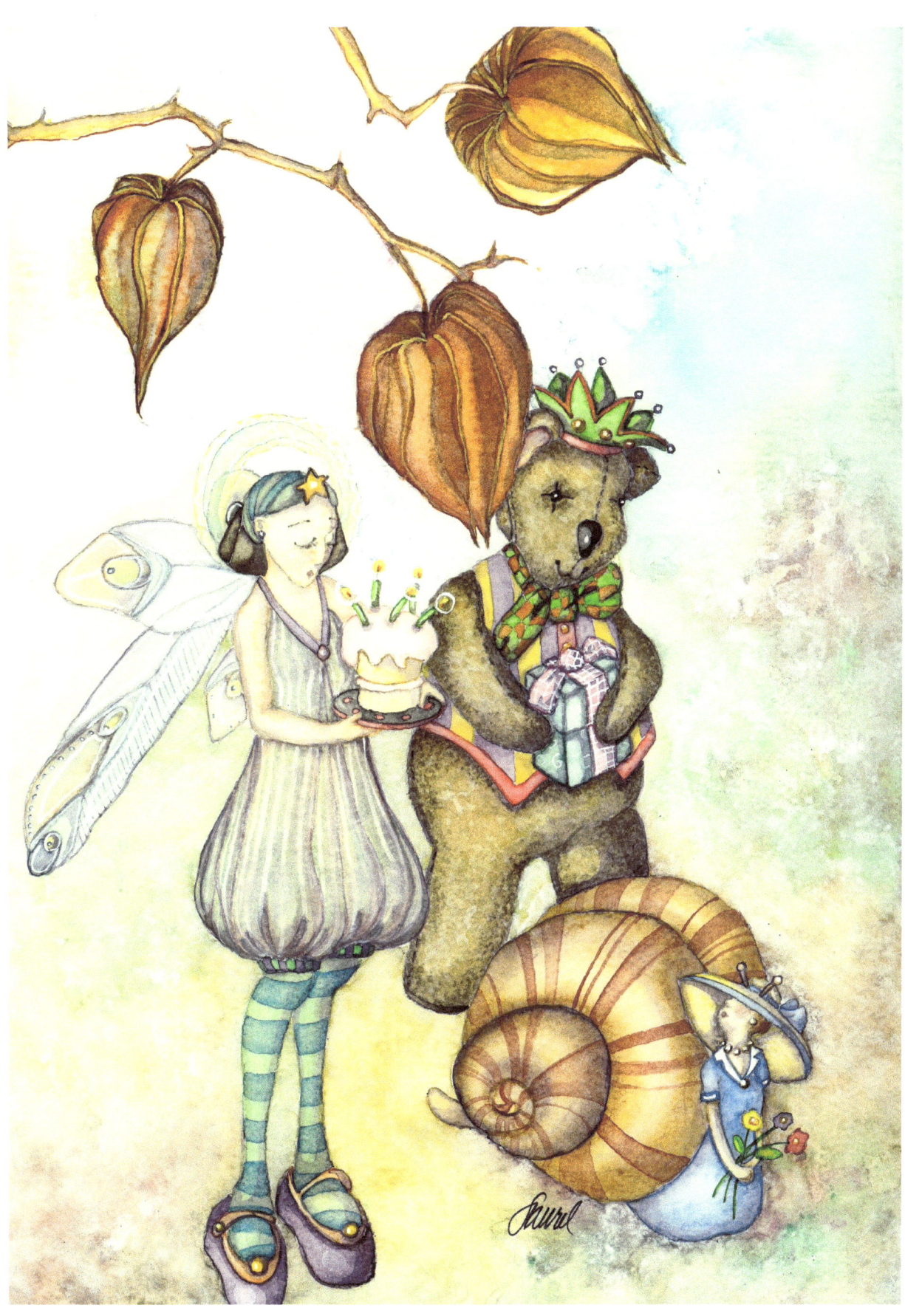

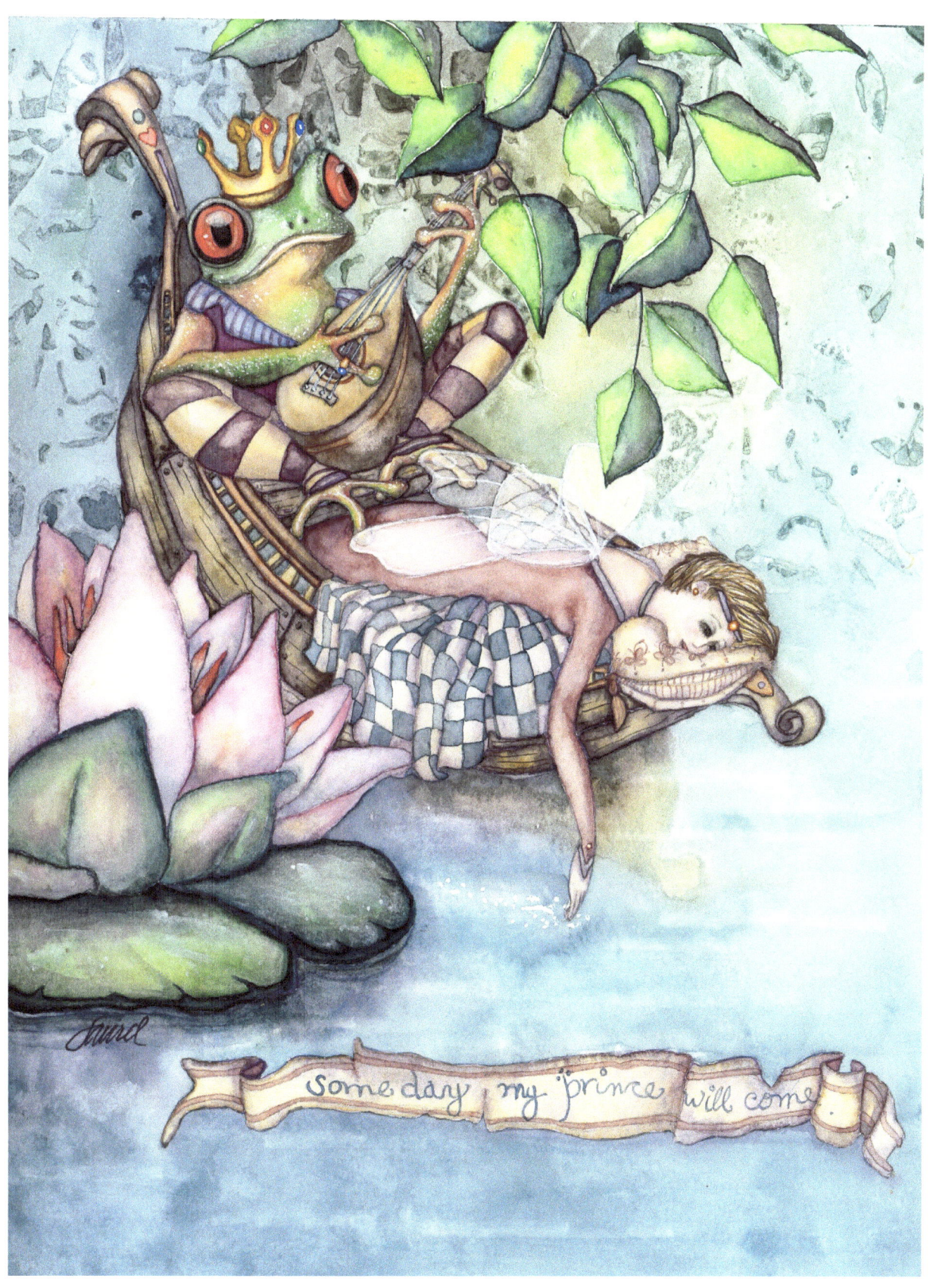

Some day my 'prince will come

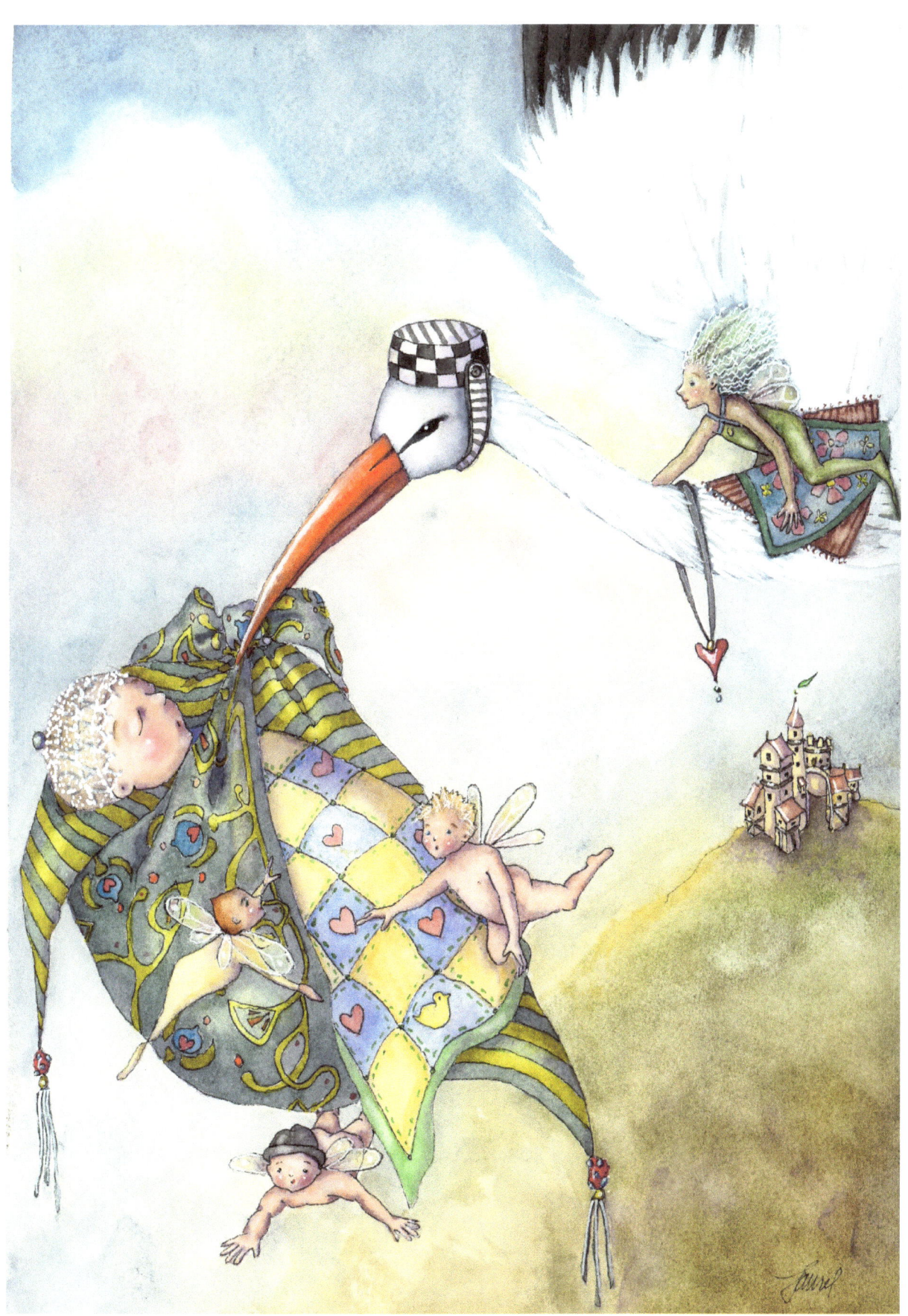

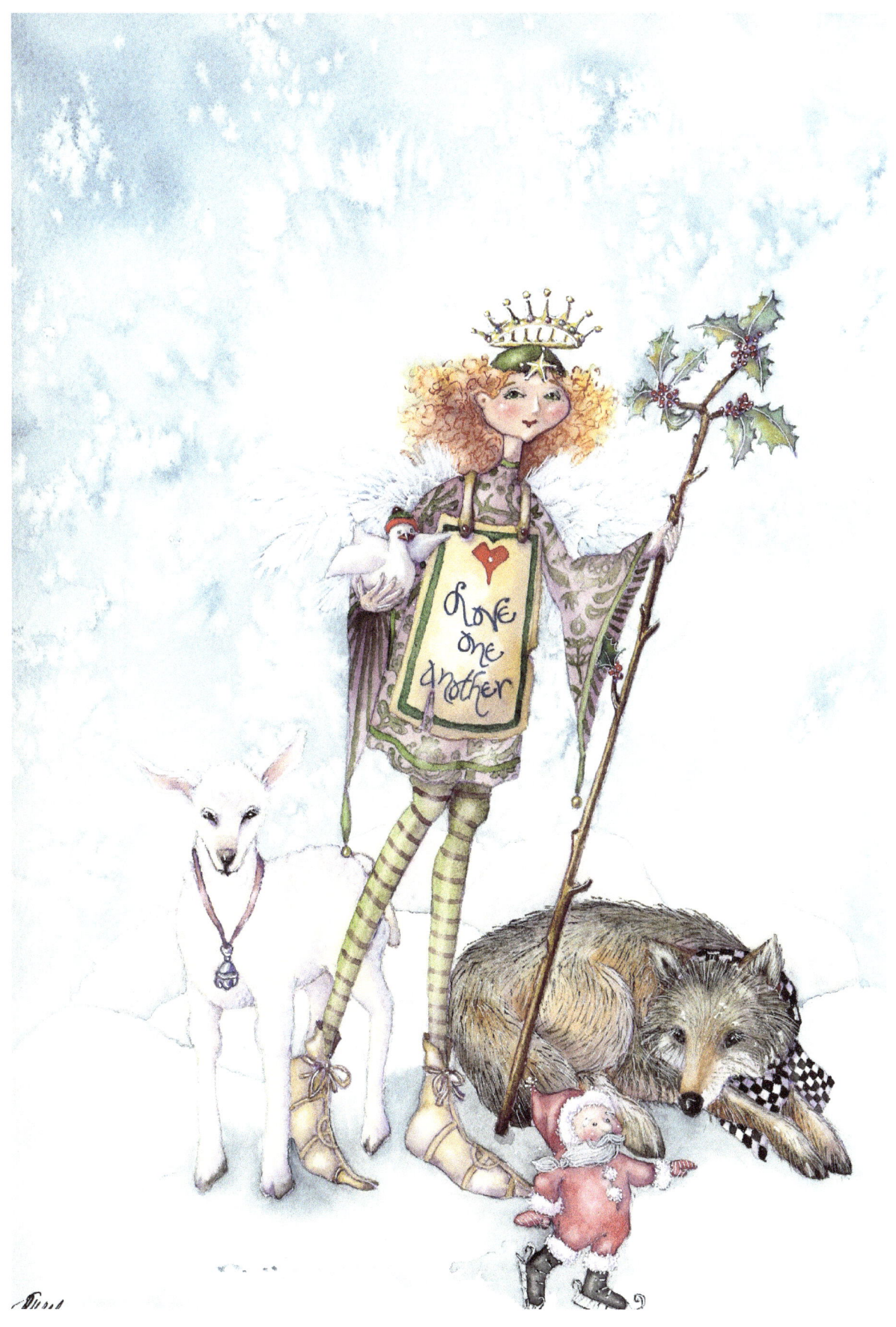

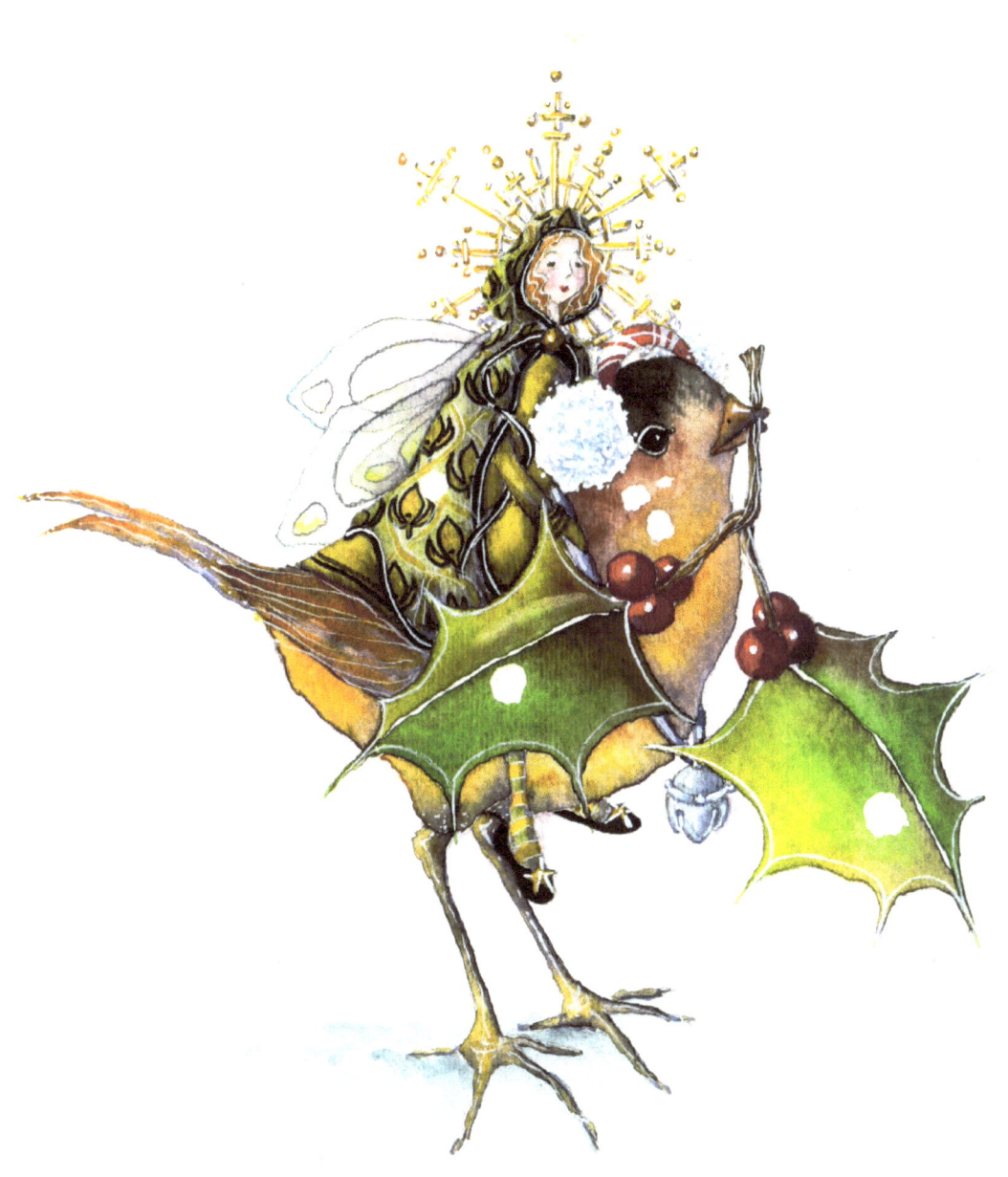

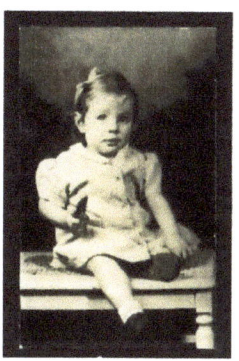

LAURELADEL@GMAIL.COM

laurelnelsonwhimsy.imagekind.com

www.ingramcontent.com/pod-product-compliance
Lightning Source LLC
Chambersburg PA
CBHW050420180526
45159CB00005B/2352